Faith and Higher Education

Mrs. H. I. Hester

Faith and Higher Education

Grady C. Cothen

Broadman Press
Nashville, Tennessee

Foreword

IN JUNE, 1971, Dr. and Mrs. H. I Hester announced the gift of an endowed lectureship for the Association of Southern Baptist Colleges and Schools, the corpus of which is to be held in perpetuity by the Southern Baptist Foundation and administered by the Education Commission.

The purpose of the endowed lectureship is to enable the Association to bring to the annual meeting each year an outstanding lecturer on Christian higher education.

Dr. Grady C. Cothen, president of the Baptist Sunday School Board, was asked to deliver the 1975 Hester Lecture Series.

Dr. Cothen has had a distinguished career as a Southern Baptist pastor, educator, and denominational leader. Prior to coming to the presidency of the Sunday School Board, he served for five years as president of New Orleans Baptist Theological Seminary. From 1966 to 1970, Dr. Cothen was president of Oklahoma Baptist University.

Because of the large number of requests for these lectures, it was the unanimous decision of the Education Commission to have them published.

The Commission and the Association of Southern Baptist Colleges and Schools are grateful to the Broadman Press for making these lectures available to the public.

The 1975 Hester Lectures are being dedicated to Mrs. H. I. Hester, who has had a lifelong interest in Southern Baptist colleges and schools and who for many years was associated with William Jewell College.

BEN C. FISHER
Executive Director
Education Commission, SBC

Preface

I WAS president of a Baptist college during the last half of the decade of the sixties. This was the era of the Vietnam War, the generation gap, the rise of the countercultures, the revolution against institutions and the birth of new expressions of old radicalisms. Higher education in those days was filled with tension which often in many places erupted into confrontation and violence. Many of the problems were introduced by or agitated by off-campus radicals.

A key change in campus life during the decade was the pressing by students for constitutional rights as guaranteed by the first amendment. As the courts ruled again and again in their favor, the colleges' legal landmark—*en loco parentis*—was swept away. The resultant loss of control of student conduct brought to the campuses a new look and feel. Anything that was legal became proper on many campuses. Tax-supported institutions particularly were immediately subjected to these findings of the courts. Such traditional student controls as dormitory hours, men visiting in women's housing and vice versa, use of the institutional facilities for political activities, et cetera, began to be abandoned.

The campuses became the recruiting ground for every "cause" in America that wanted man-woman power, idealistic young enthusiasts, intellectual prestige, and the protection of academe. Many institutions became ideological battlegrounds. Peace was a great issue and cause, and many purported to seek it with guns, knives, assaults on university officials, and burning buildings.

The public reaction, of course, was one of shock and anger. Demands were heard everywhere from the halls of Congress to the swank country clubs and boardrooms of trustees that by force, legal action, or expulsion the institutions regain control of the students. Few realized that an era was over and a new university was struggling out of the cocoon.

Baptist schools came through this period of great stress without physical violence. This represented remarkable stability. The quality of the students was revealed in their ability to deal with monumental change without resort to the radical methods of some of their peers. The faculties were sometimes provoked into political activity that involved the institution, but in the main they demonstrated remarkable reserve. Administrations were sometimes hard put to stay ahead of the rapidly veering currents of thought and action.

Yet, Baptist schools, along with the rest, were profoundly changed. Serious new legal and social directions impinged on their institutions. The accepted norms of campus life were all challenged, and some were swept away. All over again, and with new urgency, the Christian colleges must ask, "What is the essential reality that makes us different from other institutions of higher education?" Qualitative difference is more important now than ever before. With the growth of secular humanism, a return to naturalism (realism) especially in the arts, with the strong development of a new right, with the sexual revolution and the new challenges to the family, the Christian college is in a new crisis time.

The Christian school must have, understand, and use a philosophical base that is grounded in its theology. It needs to understand and explicate its presuppositions. It must be qualitatively different but must be equipped to compete intellectually with other segments of academe.

These lectures represent my own attempt to understand and articulate the nature of a Christian institution of higher education. If these papers provoke a continuing dialogue among Christian educators, I shall be grateful.

I express my gratitude to the Association of Southern Baptist Schools and Colleges for asking me to present these lectures. To Dr. and Mrs. H. I. Hester for providing for the series, all of us extend grateful thanks. To the Education Commission of the Southern Baptist Convention and to Dr. Ben Fisher, I am grateful for their publication.

GRADY C. COTHEN

1

What Is the Christian Dimension?

THERE IS perhaps more confusion on what constitutes the Christian dimension in an institution of higher education today than there is on any other single factor. It is fairly easy to define the educational dimension. It is easy to call attention to the need for the humaneness of the liberal arts, but it is extremely difficult to find adequate definitions of the Christian dimension in a college. There appears to have been little written on the subject, and even in meetings related to Christian education there is little in the way of specific definition of the Christian aspect of these institutions.

This situation obtains even though there is climate in higher education which demands commitment to some set of values. Joseph Argustfield said recently in *Danforth News and Notes,* "The intense morality and demand for sharp commitments now characteristic of student activists creates difficult dilemmas for American universities. It challenges us to create a university environment which in its characteristic style of detachment and irrelevance is nevertheless engaged and relevant. It will not be easy for administrators to become heroes and for faculties to become saints."

"Here unmistakenly we have had in the last ten years students who ask the crucial questions of human existence—identity, meaning, the existence of value, the good life—and they tend to get in response not bread but a stone. Here we have a generation blessedly capable of moral outrage, and it is the bitterest of anomalies that the humanities should be dying among students capable of moral outrage in a morally outrageous world. Almost without exception the response of universities to this profound hunger for education, for examples of human courage and compassionate intelligence, has been parochial, uncomprehending, or cold."

It seems to be true that the "how-to" generation has become the "why" generation. The generation of new rationalism has become an age of feeling. The world of scientific method is searching for humane values. Additionally, the students have been keenly interested in commitment on the part of educators to causes and values. They seem to see no incongruity between the educational dimension and the necessity for human commitment.

The most obvious repetitive note in modern students' conversation is their sense of the need for someone to care. Caring is often ill-defined, seldom carefully articulated, but the need for caring is nevertheless present. Traditional liberal arts humanistic values do not seem to be enough.

Need for Christian Values

For the welfare of modern human society there appears to be the greatest possible need for human and Christian values that are usually associated with church-related colleges. This appears at a time when in many cases the liberal arts colleges appear to try to take on as much of the nature of the multiversity as possible. Many of them seem to pride themselves in joining the parade of abrogation of values. Some rejoice that they now appear to be independent institutions without church relationship. Some of them seem to be striving for the status of the elite independent institutions with little tie to their emotional, philosophical, and spiritual heritage.

It seems therefore that a careful delineation of the nature of a Christian dimension is mandatory. If in fact these colleges are different, how are they different? Why are they different? What are the elements of difference? What are the involvements of their differences? What can be done to shore up the differences? What measures need to be adopted to make them relevant to the society in which they live? How can these differences be made to meet the needs of the students who are crying for difference?

Can these colleges in fact be qualitatively different? In an educational world where conformity seems to be the rule while innovation is the rage, it is our intent in this discussion to attempt to describe what some of these differences can be.

Distinguishing Characteristics

It is first necessary to note what a Christian dimension is not. It is not, for example, a carefully camouflaged effort at indoctrination. Indoctrination is the cry normally raised by educators when one begins to talk of spiritual values, or of Christian commitment. It is necessary to note that when you talk about the problems of Christian faith in the university context, confusion may result. Teaching students what a Christian denomination believes is often confused with teaching them what to believe. The difference is vastly significant to the process of education. For the educational purpose in a Christian institution an individual must be left to decide what he believes. It cannot be otherwise. We cannot as Christians prescribe ritual, ideal or faith for anyone. It is legitimate to teach students what Christians believe. It is not legitimate to coerce them in their personal belief.

The Christian dimension in an institution is not monastic in nature. There are those who believe that a Christian institution must insulate its students from the world in which they live. Separation from the society of evil is thought by some to be protection for young people. There are those who would interpret Christian dimension as being an effort to shield the young people for four years from the world in which they must live. In an educational institution it is not possible to isolate students from the world, nor is it desirable. The institution can be no enclave of segregation protecting the students from ideas, movements, or moods. The problems of instant communication make this impossible, even if it were desirable. Even if it were possible, it would ill-equip the young people to live in the world into which they will shortly be thrust.

The university is not a church. It should not make the mistake of functioning as a church. As we maintain intellectual and spiritual consistency, the difference in the functions must be remembered. Neither institution can usurp the functions of the other. The functions of the educational institution are those which are beyond the usual limits of the church. It is not a substitute for the church. It is not convened to judge the worthiness of ministers. The primary purpose is not evangelism. It is true that Christians within the community may evangelize. They almost certainly will gather together for cooperate worship. These are functions which are carried out because of the nature of the Christian faith, not the nature of the educational community.

Causes of Tension

Christian educators must recognize the fact that to insert the Christian dimension into an educational institution injects an entirely new set of problems. If these problems are not carefully identified, defined, and dealt with, a great deal of confusion can result in the process. There is often, for example, confusion of religion as an experience with religion as an academic discipline. Religion as a discipline must be approached with openness and honesty. All questions are legitimate. There must be willingness to accept questions that inevitably arise and an attempt to deal with them on the basis of Christian presuppositions. In short, Christianity or religion must stand on its own as must any other academic discipline.

Religion as an experience is often bolstered by religion as a discipline, but religion as an experience, in addition to the usual definitions, is a life to be lived. Christianity as an experience is a relationship to be sustained. It may include the doubts and questions of the discipline. It may run the gamut of human emotions and experiences as it involves itself concurrently as both discipline and experience, and yet the academic community must make an attempt to separate the two.

When religion is injected into the college situation, there is often confusion related to the approach to knowledge. Most of the educational system in America uses the so-called scientific approach to knowledge. It is involved basically with observation, generalization, and verification. It endlessly raises such questions as these: "How do you know? Can you reproduce the experiment? Prove it. Show me." It involves observable empirical data which can be reproduced under similar conditions. Since this is the normative approach to knowledge in the educational community, it is inevitable that certain confusions shall arise when religion becomes a part of the academic dimension. Religion is more dependent on the intuitive approach to knowledge. Revelation plays an important part in the orientation of the Christian. The Christian needs to recognize that this raises certain problems of epistemology, but he is willing to recognize the problems and deal with them in as adequate a fashion as is possible. Care must be exercised to distinguish between the approaches to knowledge. Particular emphasis should be placed on the identification of the problems which arise because of the differences in the approach to knowledge.

It should be noted in this regard that the tension between Christian faith and the intellectual world will be continuous. Things which Christians now believe from revelation are constantly brought to judgment at the bar of reason. This process will go on as long as men enter into intellectual confrontation. Christians believe that the processes of religious knowledge may very well be different. In matters of faith Christians believe and have come to know; the world wants to know first and come to believe. In science the knowing comes first and the belief second. In religion, faith comes first and then developing knowledge. The matters of faith are perceived, but in our world perception would be infinitely easier if we could understand religion both as an academic discipline and as a personal faith. There is no way to avoid the conflicts into which we are thrust except to abandon our faith. If we cannot, however, come to grips with our faith intellectually as well as in the realm of personal experience, we will lose the educated people as we may be in the process of doing already.

The Christian community must be careful to differentiate between the forms and expressions of faith and the substance of that faith. The forms of expression in Christian faith are changing. It is inevitable that young people will accelerate these changes. They are more interested in the substance of the faith than its external expressions. They are more concerned about meat than method. They are more interested in differentiating between what is externalized expression and what is internalized necessity. The methods of communication are sometimes confused with doctrinal substance within the Christian community. These are differentiations which the young people are keenly concerned about, and insist that we make.

One of the central problems with which the Christian academic community must deal is the problem of commitment versus the problems of free inquiry. It is true that there is a commitment to Christian truth, and in a Christian college it is equally true that scholars are committed to free inquiry. Is it necessary that these two seemingly variant positions be incompatible? True scholars are committed to freedom of inquiry, and true Christians are committed to Christian truth. To many people these two apparently opposing stances pose serious problems. The true scholar is willing to have his presuppositions debated and examined. It is also true that all education involves some set of presuppositions. In education the Christian must be willing to examine his own presuppositions and values.

The necessary openness is thus for both the Christian and the scholar desirable and demanded. The committed Christian must take his place in the intellectual arena with the assurance that Christ and the Scriptures are capable of standing examination. To attempt to maintain a Christian position by lack of openness or by outright oppression is both unchristian and unsound educationally. On the other hand, to say that commitment is educationally impossible is to deny the facts that everywhere exist. There does not seem to be any essential incompatibility between these two positions properly understood. This point of view presumes that demonstrated error might change opinions arrived at by open inquiry or conceivably, theoretically, could change the position of committed Christians. In any case, the two stances must be maintained if the educational institution is to fulfil its purposes educationally and spiritually.

What Then Is the Christian Dimension?

In setting forth the nature of the Christian dimension in an educational institution, it is essential that the institution recognize its own statement of philosophy and purposes, and that it clearly enunciate the presuppositions on which it operates and which undergird the school. This statement must involve more than lip service. These philosophical positions must be active forces in institutional policy. They must be the basis for academic judgment. In short, if the institution is to be spiritually and educationally sound, there must be an honest and intelligent attempt to be what it says it is.

One element of the Christian dimension is surely an atmosphere which is conducive to faith. The discussion of the ultimate nature of Christian and spiritual values must be offered in an atmosphere that makes possible their serious consideration. This will involve the influence of people who are dedicated to Christ and learning. It involves guidance and counseling. It involves an atmosphere in which it is easy to talk about eternal verities, the nature of God, and other such subjects.

This community was recently described by Dr. William Mitchell, professor of English and now dean of the College of Liberal Arts at Oklahoma Baptist University as "an atmosphere which reflects the virtues of Christian tenants: namely, love and respect for one's fellowman, responsibility in words and actions, zeal in the search for truth and knowledge, integrity, humility, reverence for and faith in God, and belief that each person has purpose in his life's actions."

Demonstration of Christian qualities in life is crucially important to the maintenance of Christian dimension in an educational institution. Among other things, this will mean a restraint on conduct that outrages Christian conscience. It means a general observance of Christian moral and ethical standards, not by reason of coercion, but by reason of personal commitment to these standards.

Another element in the Christian dimension is the quality of persons who are present in the community. It is essential for the Christian dimension that these be committed Christian people. This involves more than agreement with the goals of humaneness. This means Christian people who try to live the life. It means people who are committed to Christian values. These are people who will be interested in the goals of the institution. They are people who will be willing to accept such limitations as the Christian community requires. They will be committed to the interests and the needs of young people. It is perhaps in the quality of the people involved in the process that Christian education finds its greatest ally. Without a quality of life which demonstrates Christian commitment, it is unlikely that young people will become seriously interested in this dimension of life.

An element of the Christian dimension is a fair and honest treatment of the Christian faith. This means a recognition of the validity of the Christian religion as a discipline. It means a fair and honest presentation in the classroom of the tenets of the Christian faith. It means the responsible treatment in honesty and fairness of the Christian religion in chapel, in the focus week observances, etc. It means that there will be no intellectual slighting or minimizing of the faith if it is to be a true dimension in the institution itself.

It means, of course, devotion to God and to the church. Of particular significance to young people in this kind of society is devotion to Christian attitudes toward people. The entire structure of the community, including all the elements of the Christian dimension which have been mentioned, rides on the generation of Christian attitudes. Further, this element means a Christian commitment to colleagues and students, involving the practice of Christian caring in the human relationships of the Christian community.

A Christian Community

The Christian dimension means the establishing and maintenance of a Christian community. This is perhaps one of the most difficult tasks involved in the problems of Christian higher education today. It requires the highest quality of Christian leadership. It will certainly begin with the president, who must understand and sponsor the creation and maintenance of a Christian community. All administrative officers who deal with disciplinary and academic problems must be committed to these values. The faculty, together with the administration, must understand the nature of a Christian community. All of these officers of a college must be dedicated to its creation and its maintenance. It will not be born accidentally. It will not thrive on neglect. There must be leaders who will show by their conduct the viability of the Christian ideals in life.

One of the crucial elements in a Christian community in today's world will be the obvious respect for the dignity of individuals. One of the great needs in human relationships today is the recognition of the inherent worth and dignity of each individual, and respect for his uniqueness. These principles are rooted and founded in the Christian faith. Their observance and use will be one of the most attractive ways of presenting the Christian faith possible in this kind of world.

This means basically caring for the interests and concerns of other people. It means a willingness to become involved with them in their needs, whether they be personal or academic. It means concern for the individual when there is a problem related to courses, courtship difficulties, expressions of rebellion and all of the other crises—it means an interest in dropouts, in failing students, in the problems of academics and the problems of personal lives. There is no place in this kind of community for people who want to do only research or teach a few hours. There is no place in this community for the philosophy that it would be great to be a college teacher if there were no students.

The maintenance of a Christian community requires that due process be available for all members of the community. It means the assurance that justice and equity are available. It involves adequate opportunity for defense. If under the law, due process must be assured to students in the public school, the Christian community can certainly do no less.

The tools of the community of Christians are those of reason. This community must be maintained by "sweet reason," as much as this is possible. The tools of reason—argumentation and dialogue—are those which will be daily employed within the confines of the community. There cannot be any coercion in the matters of intellect. Coercion will be a tool of the academic Christian community only as it is necessary to maintain the integrity and the health of the community. The uses of power must be limited to those essential to the creation and maintenance of valid academic life. Rules will be limited to those necessary to make possible a Christian dimension.

In short, this community cannot exist as long as disruption of the academic process or personal rights of any member of the community is allowed. Of necessity, there must be some limitations on the overtly unchristian conduct of the members of community. In part, these limitations must be accepted voluntarily. In part, they must be enforced to prevent the supporting society from turning on this unique community. This will mean that Christian ethical and moral standards will be presented and defended, though openness concerning them and their practice must be a part of the community. In short, the Christian community means a constant and consistent application of Christian principles in human relationships by all members of the community.

It is recognized, of course, that many students will not be competent in these areas. Many faculty people will not be interested in the rather rigorous strictures. Yet if Christian higher education is to survive in this kind of world, this sort of community must be attempted and these fundamental precepts must be involved.

The Christian community is a place of commitment to each person and a commitment to the institution. The community of interests between faculty and students must be real. The faculty must be thus concerned about the genuine total welfare of the student. They should be interested in it, and committed to it. Students must feel that the institutional welfare is their responsibility and be committed to it.

This inevitably involves the sense of Christian ministry to students. Certainly students will not always conduct themselves as they should. This is the point at which ministry involves itself in the community. It will be essential for the academicians to help students work their way through personal problems. This will involve all the problems of maturation, the choice of a profession, and the selection of a life mate. Interest in the student will involve his religious crisis, his adoption of a lifestyle, and his setting the course of his life. Christian commitment means the helping of students in the intellectual struggle caused by the pluralism in the educational world and society in which they live. It will help them understand religion as a discipline and its relationship to their personal faith.

Synthesis of Knowledge

One of the most crucial problems facing the church-related institution of higher education and its Christian community is the necessity to attempt some synthesis of knowledge.

A Christian dimension should assist in the development of a stance from which reality can be viewed comprehensively. The inevitable question of course is: "Is this possible?" Christians believe that it is, that such a stance can be developed and is broad enough to include responsibly the sciences, social sciences, and humanities. Christians believe that it should deal with the facts of man and his history, and that the Christian faith will offer some explanation of man and his behavior, his hopes and his weaknesses. In short, the Christian institution should be involved in the attempt to help the student with world view.

The college must press this point. It would perhaps be the Christian institution's greatest contribution if this program can be adequately developed. It offers great potential in the realm of the uniqueness of the institution and its educational and spiritual goals.

A constant vision of the ideal of Christian community is essential. It must be magnified, dramatized, planned, promoted and lived. The objectives are worthy of the cost. The achieving of this Christian community may in fact be the only way this type of higher education can survive.

Requirements of a Christian Academic Community

McKenzie and Patillo said in the preface to their volume, "It will become clear we believe that the most basic problem of church sponsored higher education is in a very real sense theological. The shifting sands of religious faith today provide an uncertain foundation for religiously oriented educational programs. Our proposals for action do not, indeed cannot, solve this central problem. There is no way to manufacture agreement on fundamental questions. What we have to do is present as distinctly as possible the theological dilemma of church affiliated institutions of higher education. It is inconceivable that such an institution can exist without squarely facing the problem of its theological basis. What is its theology? What are its involvements? What are the intellectual implications of the Christian faith as stated by the theology of the particular institution."[1]

The theological base of an institution raises serious questions. Given a theology, we have to ask: Are the apparent conflicts in our world of knowledge real or superficial? What does faith mean in the academic world? What is the relation of the Christian faith to the knowledge of other types? What problems do modern sociological studies pose for Christian faith? What is the relationship of psychological insights to revealed truth? What does anthropology say to Christian presuppositions? Philosophy and theology—do they speak to the needs of men today? How? Do they vary from the revealed truth in the New Testament? These are questions which are inevitable and desirable.

The Christian institution must meet squarely the challenge of the disciplines to faith. For example, it is said that it is difficult to find a graduate school in philosophy in this country that "takes the idea of God seriously." A nontheistic philosophy will inevitable raise serious questions to Christians. Various schools of psychology and sociological fads pose real problems. Science, in its varied and ever-changing explanations of how things came to be as they are, poses anthropological and cosmological questions to Christians. One of the central responsibilities of a Christian institution and its Christian dimension is that it must meet squarely these challenges. Most seem to do a poor job in this particular area. Intellectual honesty demands, however, that some attempt be made to deal with these problems which the disciplines raise.

The Christian dimension of an institution must speak to the issues of the society. A distinctly Christian voice should be heard on the problems of students. The problems of society at large have grave implications for Christians and their theology. Much can be said for a Christian college and its need to speak with a

---

[1]McKenzie and Patillo, *Church Sponsored Higher Education in the United States of America*, Council on Education, preface, VII.

reasoned view of war and peace, and the issues of poverty and race, and whatever else plagues mankind.

These are large orders. This is an idealistic purpose, and yet it is essential to hold up the ideal and endlessly to work toward it. These may very well be termed to be some of the goals of Christian higher education. The Christian college, if it is to be meaningful in the modern world of education, must be honest with itself, its constituent members, and those publics which relate to it. The institution will need to be distinctly Christian in its orientation. It will need to make proper provision for the creation and maintenance of a Christian community. It will have to meet squarely the intellectual conflicts of its day. It is an exciting and exhilarating task, and worthy of the best that is in Christian educators.

2

Inundation by Society

THE PROBLEMS of the society in which we live, not directly related to education, are making survival of Christian higher education much more difficult. Many of these problems are endlessly thrusting themselves into college life. The conflicts of society and the polarization about many present-day issues create almost impossible situations for the Christian college. Many of the groups fostering various social changes demand that the colleges follow them. These groups are often at opposite poles. Since they insist that the colleges follow their wishes, very difficult situations are created.

Many of these conflicts strike Christian higher education at its most vulnerable points. Some of them are crucial to the public relations needs of the college. Some challenge the basic philosophic stances of the institutions. Church-related higher education is in particularly poor position to defend itself against these forces.

The changes in the patterns of society threaten to destroy Christian higher education completely. On the other hand, if these forces can be met and dealt with, the resultant climate should be good for the growth and development of qualitatively different higher education. The issue, basically, is to survive in a society that is basically antithetical in many of its positions to the philosophical base of the Christian college. The college must survive in this atmosphere and somehow attempt to change it.

A Revolutionary Society

Many serious social observers are calling present-day society revolutionary in nature. One such formulation of our society is contained in a study on campus tensions. Dr. Keniston holds that a true revolution is going on in our society. He says in part, "First, I believe that what are euphemistically called campus tensions result in a considerable part from social and historical changes and political administrative policies which do not originate primarily in the colleges and universities. Much of the turbulence in highly industrialized society stems from the too highly explosive social revolutions that are simultaneously under way. The first is the ancient process of inclusion in the industrial society—what Ralph Dorendorf has termed the extension of citizenship. The first revolution involves the demand that American society include as full citizens many persons who have traditionally been excluded from the mainstream of social, economic and political life, those who are not white, adult, middle class, Protestant, Anglo-Saxon and male. Thus from blacks, young people, women, Jews and Catholics and a variety of ethnic groups and working lower-class individuals, we hear evermore striving demands to be counted in as full members of society, granted full legal rights in equal psychocultural esteem. Because the rhetoric of American society is the rhetoric of a democracy in full citizenship, and because of the high levels of material abundance, social security and formal political freedom in our society, the demand for inclusion has today become more clamorous and insistent.

"But overlapping, and to some extent opposing this first trend, are the less articulate but strongly felt demands of those who form part of a second revolution. This revolution, less sociopolitical than psychocultural, occurs in the children of those who have made it in the existing system; children of intellectuals, professionals, high-level government administrators, market researchers in the cosmopolitan upper middle class of America, France, West Germany, Japan and so on. For such men and women, most of them young, the promises of the first revolution seem already fulfilled. Citizenship is attained, inclusion is assured. The new questions that arise for such young men and women concern the meaning and quality of life in a post-industrial setting; their first provisional answers emphasize qualitative transformation, a rejection of the human, bureaucratic, ecological price paid to attain high levels of industrialization, a search for fulfillment and more intense experience and an effort to achieve new forms of intimacy, awareness, and community."[1]

However one formulates the discussion of the revolutionary society, there seems to be little question that these struggles are real and that the structures of society are under constant assault. These struggles are basically intellectual in nature as well as social. It is inevitable, therefore, that the colleges and universities should be involved in them at all levels. It is equally inevitable that the Christian institution searching for truly human values and attempting to live up to the ethical standards of the Christian faith will find itself embroiled in a struggle which is as basically human as these conflicts which have been mentioned.

Permissive Society

It is quite obvious that society is moving in its patterns of control from authoritarianism to freedom. The problems related to what is authority and who is authority are everywhere evident in the American society. Nowhere do these impinge on human life more surely than in the college and university setting.

Marcus G. Raskin said in *Perspectives on Campus Tensions*, that these crises are basic and major. "There are two major and basic crises in the university. The first is a reflection of a political crisis that now manifests itself across the entire American society, the crises in political authority. To put it another way: By what authority does A tell B what is wrong or right? By what authority does A tell B what to do? By what authority does A get to control his lifetime and B cannot? In the university this crisis manifests itself in efforts by groups hitherto unconscious of themselves to ask what authority others have over them, where their legitimacy comes from and who granted it to them. Such questions—they are ones endemic to the next generation—will force a redrafting of the social contract before 2000 in our major institutions, including the body politic itself. The problem of redrafting the

---

[1]Kenneth Keniston, "What's Bugging The Students?" *Perspectives on Campus Tensions*, American Council on Education, 1970.

social contract is especially acute in the university since its ideology and rhetoric (but not the reality) assure us that authority, legitimacy and truth derive from verification and persuasion, not magic, threat, force, who rules, or delayed payoff."

As patterns of authority are constantly being changed, society has moved rapidly toward a permissive philosophy not held so pervasively in America before. The generation of Spock babies reared in a permissive atmosphere have now asserted their rights in every area. Society is rapidly accepting changing moral values. The sexual revolution is everywhere evident. Language formerly unacceptable in mixed company is now a regular feature on prime-time television. The rapid deterioration of so many homes, the ease and frequency of divorce, and the rise of overt immorality all signal added difficulties for the Christian college. One study shows that the number of unmarried couples living together has increased 800 percent in 10 years. The number of households headed by singles is up 55 percent in the decade. Forty percent of marriages now end in divorce, and 50 percent of those under age 34.

With the rapid leeching out from society of Christian norms, the quality of the students is sure to change. The growth of the drug culture, the high rise in crime, the inordinate emphasis on freedom without responsibility all contribute to the rapid erosion of the Christian values in the society. These changes are seriously affecting the colleges' moral climate. The fact is illustrated in the problem of the demand for unlimited dormitory visitation rights by both male and female students. Dress regulations in colleges everywhere are virtually a thing of the past. The rules of conduct are under endless assault. Hours for women controlled by the institution are rapidly disappearing as a more permissive society demands complete freedom with little in the way of limitations on personal conduct.

The rapid rise of violence and crime in the public schools, including the assaults on teachers, principals, and security guards, will pose new threats to peace and order in the Christian college. A generation of students educated amid physical danger will likely react on a different level to the tensions of college adjustment.

The social promotion theories that pass everyone through the high schools without requiring basic knowledge and skills will contribute to the unrealistic expectations of the uneducated.

When one adds to all of this the fact that students will increasingly come from disordered segments of society and broken homes, the problems of the colleges may increase geometrically.

Permissiveness either gives rise to, or reinforces, reactionary forces that have become increasingly active. Large segments of the population are more comfortable in the old patterns of authority. They hold still to a more rigid code of sexual conduct and are generally more conservative in their approach to social values. These segments of society have not accepted the radical changes with any degree of grace and are resisting with increasing vigor. Groups of social vigilantes are rising everywhere. Organizations within society to protect older values are becoming more clamorous in their demand that their rights and opinions be respected. Varying right-wing elements in society are intensifying their efforts to regain control of a society which they feel is slipping from their grasp.

B. F. Skinner in *Beyond Freedom and Dignity* argues that "our concepts of freedom and dignity must be sharply revised. The environment must be changed rather than man himself if the traditional goals are to be achieved. In his thinking the technology of behavior comes out of the shadows and onto the table for discussion."

These reactionary forces are increasingly active in education. In the name of Americanism and religion they are pressing colleges to maintain the positions of the 40's and the 50's.

Christian higher education, particularly, is caught between these warring forces. Constituents of the Christian college may very well fall in both camps. Varying ideologies are held by differing segments of the community. Colleges historically have tried to appeal to these persons in the name of Christian moral and ethical values to support the institutions and have succeeded to some degree. Thus in the present milieu, the Christian institution is suffering from both its friends and its enemies.

A Participatory Society

Closely akin to the problems of the permissive society are those which relate to society's request for participation by all of its elements in the decision-making process. The demand to share authority over the affairs of their lives is everywhere heard from all groups. Raskin, in "What Is the New University?" says: "For a body politic to be acceptable to those living within its domain, the authority must be shared in a way that is acceptable to its citizens. Take a symbolic example: Why should a president of a university be chosen by a board of trustees? The choice of the president of the university is something which involves the entire membership of the university community. Through a system of voting and participation it would be possible for students, faculty, workers, researchers and administrators to participate in choosing a president. This procedure would help in changing the perception of the student as having no part in the government of the institution in which he shall live."[2]

The demand to share in participation in the affairs of the college is now frequently being put on the basis of the right of a citizen under the law to share in his own destiny. Again Raskin says, "For a young person, the university rights of citizenship would relate to him as a full member of a political community in which he has rights to privacy against self-incrimination, freedom of speech and action, as well as sexual freedom. The university community would give new meaning to the Federal Bill of Rights and undertake to set a community to fulfill these rights. The Bill of Rights would no longer be merely a formal political matter between the state and the individual."[3] Cognizance is being taken of the fact that corporate power has abrogated political rights.

The participatory philosophy takes many differing directions. Recently in a meeting of the Executive Committee of the SBC, students were invited to sit in on the meeting and participate as they desired. It was a business session dealing with many millions of dollars, and with the future of a considerable number of

---

[2]Raskin, op. cit., p. 36.
[3]Ibid., p. 34.

institutions. As the students sat through these meetings participating as members of the deliberative body, it was obvious that speeches were suffering from being undelivered. At the close of the meeting, upon invitation, one girl stood to say, "I've had many things on my heart about various matters in our denominational life. I have had no opportunity to say them."

It had eluded her altogether that this was a meeting not for the expression of opinion, but for the transaction of business. This was not a platform to be provided for anyone to express views on the difficulties of the society in which we live. Her concept of participation included the idea that the affairs of a very large denomination and of many busy professional people must be delayed while she made speeches on varying subjects as she desired. This is an extreme example, to be sure, and yet it is evidence of the problems of involvement in a participating society.

It is a truism that those segments of society which demand the right to participate in decision-making process are of varying opinions. These participants are of unequal ability in thought and articulation. They have unequal comprehension and are from widely varying backgrounds. Obviously, not all of these people can have their way. A net effect for the educational institution is that it becomes a platform for social interaction and provides innumerable opportunities for confusion. Social forces are injected into the decision-making processes of the institutions. Legal battles are fought in the forum of the educational institutions. A growing body of legal problems necessitates either a lawyer for president, or the ready availability of counsel.

This situation creates an endless struggle on the part of administrations to protect the decision-making process while problems of authority and participation are being solved. The procedures involve so much time and consultation as on occasion to freeze the institutional decision-making process and produce chaos. Under such circumstances many of these battles are being fought, and it is sometimes difficult to make a viable decision.

In the decision-making process in this country, it is often essential to use a representative form of governance to avoid some of the cumbersome machinery of a pure democracy. One of the problems in the present demand to participate is that the participation sought is not on a representative basis, but on the basis of direct democratic procedure during which the individual demanding his rights may appear before ultimate authority. While this may appear to be a great stride forward in the process of participation, it may have a deadly effect on the decision-making processes. Such forces are constantly challenging traditional stances of the institution and the statement of purposes of the college. There is endless argument about philosophy and about relationships within the structure. All of this may be healthy social interaction, but it makes decision-making in an educational institution extremely cumbersome.

The Impingement of Causes

Of great importance during these times to the Christian college are the ideological battles of society. Endlessly the struggles of America are impinging on the college, its autonomy and its decision-making processes.

During the last decade American society, as is well known, has been in severe struggle over many issues. Racism came to be a byword as well as a favorite ideological battleground. The war in Viet Nam was seized upon by many campus and other forces as being an issue over which bloodshed in the cause of peace was justified. Social programs of government including the attack on poverty have attracted much attention and great allegiance. Crime thrives in every metropolitan center, and law and order have become favorite catch words of politicians. Social values in the country are far from stable and produce increasing conflict in many segments of society.

In the last decade many of the causes represented by these conflicts found support on college campuses from both faculty and students. These are problems and factors in which students and faculty are interested. Ideas are the raw material of education. Youthful enthusiasm furnishes a volatile source of excitement and support.

Most organizers of movements gravitated toward college campuses. Many confrontations were produced on the campuses and in society through manipulation of students and faculty.

The Viet Nam moratorium of 1969 is an example of an idea originated by nonstudents which found its basic support on the college campuses. The education enterprise in America was seriously concerned with this effort and was for a considerable period of time polarized around this issue. While the so-called years of apathy are upon us, there is some evidence that causes may be moving back to the campus.

In the past, these movements have achieved a degree of stature and respectability by their association with the institutions of higher education. Professional people found on the college campuses are often personally involved in social, political, and economic movements. The ferment of ideas within the college furnishes fertile ground for confrontation. Intellectual combat is already a way of life. There is the legitimizing power of the college or university structure. There is already existent, as though it were ready-made for the purpose, the strong power base which the educational institution furnishes to those who have a cause to promote.

These forces have produced enormous pressures within the university communities to politicize the institution. Too often they have been successful.

The very nature of an institution of higher education involves it in social, political, and economic interests of the country. External forces which would use it for the reasons stated will likely pressure the college again. When activism regenerates as a way of life, the college will almost surely be its home.

In the last decade the revolutionaries were trying to radicalize the institution. The conservatives were attempting to capture it. The educational institution was caught in the middle of its various publics and pulled from every side and threatened by the very people who created it. Its purposes were being seriously threatened by the varying groups in society who want to use it for their own purposes.

These problems are particularly difficult for the Christian institution, since it has a commitment to a system of values, to ethical standards, and to moral principles. Much of this commitment is to social justice. On the other hand, the commitment is also to orderly process. With the tugging and pulling of society on all sides, it is extremely difficult to communicate the true nature of the institution and its commitment.

Societal Expectations and Legal Limitations

Several curious conflicts occur in this social situation in American higher education. Society, in many instances, still expects the kind of conduct from colleges and universities that existed in earlier days. It is expected that student activism will be controlled by strong administrators, and often that students will be prevented from participating in the confrontations of the day.

As is well known to this audience, for generations in this country student conduct on and off campus has traditionally depended on a legal doctrine called *in loco parentis*. This is an idea that means basically that the institutions act for the parent in the relationship with the student. This doctrine gave to the institution immediate control of the student and easier management of problems in the context of the educational institution. This process has changed radically.

Bolding says in his chapter on "Fundamental Considerations" in *Perspectives*, "In regard to the relation of the student to the university we find movements in divergent directions. *In loco parentis* has become extremely unpopular and seems to be in the process of being abandoned. We no longer pretend that the university is one big happy family and the students are children. The students have increasingly insisted on the right to their private lives as witnessed by the growing unpopularity of dormitories, the tendency for students to move into apartments where they are not subject to regulations, and the general assumption that by the time a student comes to the university he is an adult and no longer needs parental supervision is increasing in popularity. The abandonment of *in loco parentis* indeed seems to be satisfactory to everybody. The university gets out from under the troublesome and disagreeable responsibility, and the student achieves an adult freedom. There is not much evidence that he abuses freedom more than older adults. *In loco parentis* in a sense assumes that there is a great moral improvement with age, an assumption for which the evidence is a bit skimpy."[4] One point which Dr. Bolding does not take into account in this connection is that parents and often other segments of society do not agree with his doctrine of the happiness of everyone over the abandonment of the ancient practice. The Baptist public sometimes demands that the college act as parent even when the legal authority is at best questionable.

It is quite obvious that the colleges are moving from isolation to involvement. There seems to be a cultural lag between student conduct and the public expectations. Much of the society still expects the students and faculty to follow patterns of reserved conduct of another day. When problems arise, administrations are expected to handle the matters promptly, and off-campus problem conduct is no exception. The public does not understand often why the administration does not promptly dismiss offenders.

To understand these difficulties it is necessary to understand the present insistence by students, their attorneys, sometimes their parents, and by the promoters of causes on the observance of the civil rights of the student.

Thus with the student and sometimes parental insistence that the civil rights of the individual be observed, court action related to university control of conduct is always a possibility. The courts have made clear that at least in the public institutions civil rights of students may not be violated. Due attention must be given to assure that the legal requirements are met in dealing with students. Most legal authorities believe that these rulings will apply soon to private institutions. Some of you already are involved in these struggles.

From this limited discussion it is obvious that there are increasing demands for due process under the law. In other words, students are now insisting that the legal values and protections of general society become a part of the management of the college community. In offenses against the college community the administration must now allow formal legal procedures

---

[4]Bolding, "Fundamental Considerations," *Perspectives on Campus Tensions,* American Council on Education, 1970.

which insure society's idea of justice. This will certainly include the presence of counsel, keeping of records, sufficient time to prepare cases and all of the other involvements of legal process. It is equally obvious that a great deal of time and effort must be consumed upon these problems and that the colleges are becoming more and more deeply involved in legal processes.

This means that machinery and personnel must be maintained to insure that the college's legal position is not jeopardized by illegal conduct in the control of students. Basically, this may very well mean that anything which goes in the general society will now go in a college community. This will make Christian higher education very difficult to maintain.

The body of administrative decisions by the federal bureaucracy increasingly encroaches on all of the institutions of society. The Equal Employment Opportunity Commission is constantly grinding out regulations and controls that have the force of law. Certain of these decisions portend real problems for the Christian school. For example, one denominational agency has been informed that it cannot fire pregnant women who have no husbands. Divorcees have been declared a minority who have the right to continued employment even though adultery was the cause of the divorce.

Such rulings threaten the confidence of the constituency in institutions. If it becomes impossible to maintain a stance of moral and ethical integrity, the Christian institution will be in serious jeopardy from the view of its character and its public relations.

Secularization of Student and Faculty

Whether these factors are cause or effect is not here important. The forces previously discussed are radically changing the nature of the college community. One of these forces is the secularization of the minds of students and faculty. Dr. Kenneth Scott Latourette, church historian, said shortly before his death to a national gathering of denominational and educational leadership. "The first portion of a Christian college to become secularized is its student body. The faculty soon follows the secularization process."

These are often the same young people who do not subscribe to the value system of their parents and who have lost touch with the churches. Yet, these are the students who very often desire the excellence of many of the independent institutions of higher education. These are the students and faculty members who, with a largely secular orientation, are interested in changing the institutions which were founded for different purposes.

The Changing Shape of Christian Higher Education

These forces are changing the shape of Christian higher education in this country. It is especially difficult for the Christian institution to maintain its integrity amidst these surging forces. In the more conservative Christian society, these forces may create a severe reaction to student secularity and changing moral values. Many patterns of student and/or faculty conduct may not be commensurate with Christian ethics.

In these conditions public relations problems for Christian higher education are particularly difficult. There is no possibility of ivory towerism for Christian institutions. They are immediately responsible to their constituency, and there is no legislative body between them. The Christian college is strongly dependent on good relationships with its constituency.

Thus the forces of society may very well inundate the Christian college with change that it does not want, or cannot handle. In some cases the colleges are going along with the societal and educational changes and trying to blend in with the demands of changing structures. It is extremely difficult to hold on to both worlds. Christian values are often at wide variation with the values of society. Thus, the conflicts between segments of the students and faculty as well as constituency intensify.

Add one other consideration. Liberal arts education is considered by increasing numbers as an unnecessary variant in a highly technologized society. Graduates seem to have increasing difficulty in finding work in a tight job market. Specific technical skills are at a premium in these days, with multitudes unappreciative of the need for general education. Marketable skills are particularly attractive in times of recession. Educational balance may be increasingly difficult to maintain.

The Christian institution will be hard put to maintain: (1) its educational validity; (2) its own purpose for existence; (3) sound fiscal management; (4) good public relations which are essential to its existence. If the societal pressures continue to intensify, and if they are not clearly understood by the Christian constituency, the maintenance and integrity of the institutions will be impossible. It is difficult enough at best to obtain unity, cohesion, and educational integrity. The surging tides of societal change may very well sweep the Christian institution away. This is occurring at a time when the values of the Christian institution are most seriously needed by all segments of the society.

You will note that the classic problem of the Christian college—money—has not been considered. The most hazardous encroachment may not come by way of frontal assault. The Christian school may suffer most from the rising waters of an inundating society.

3

A Working Model of a Christian College

FOR THE Christian college the danger of inundation by the rising tide of a secular society is a present reality. But this is not the whole story. If your college has a true Christian dimension, you possess one of the most attractive hopes in higher education. There is a market for your product and a hunger for the reaffirmation of your values. Indeed most of your schools are stronger now than they have ever been.

Careful attention to reality and a working model of a Christian college can make possible for your schools their best days. I would like to suggest the major outlines of a model for a Christian college that I believe can thrive in the hostile soil of today's world.

The institution must be designed according to a carefully articulated plan. It must be a conscious creation of a critical mind.

One of the problems in Christian higher education today is that too much has been left to chance, or like Topsy, "Things have just growed." In the case of existing institutions in order to achieve the objectives here outlined, various aspects of the institution should be consciously reshaped to meet the requirements of the model.

Philosophy

Logically, we should begin at the beginning with the discussion of the philosophical basis of the institution. It must begin with the essential involvement of its theology. One of the requirements of the model is that it must face its own theology, and must state it as clearly and succinctly as is possible. There must be a frank recognition that the institution exists because of these Christian presuppositions. This essential step is basic to the entire process of the formulation of philosophical goals and the establishing of a qualitatively different institution. The statement of Christian theology is basic to Christian human relationships. To leave a Christian institution of higher education to depend upon the humaneness of liberal arts is to disfranchise it from the beginning.

The theological statement need not necessarily be a creedal statement nor specifically confessional.

Dare an institution state its theology? If it does, some problem will arise; if it does not, it will surely suffer from the uncertainties of a nebulous foundation. Why not say it? God is. Christ is the revealer of God. The Scriptures present a record of his dealing with man. The Scriptures mirror the mind of Christ on the relationships of man to God, to himself, and to his fellow beings. This statement is not a doctrinal statement on the Bible but suggests a basis on which to establish a norm by which to measure the functioning of the institution.

If God is the Creator, and man is the creature, and if the physical world is from God, his command to subdue the earth opens all of the doors to honest inquiry and the pursuit of truth related to the entire creation.

The philosophy of Christian higher education can begin with a theology that begins with faith in God and a commitment to Jesus Christ. There is involved a commitment to Christian ideals, particularly as they are related to interpersonal human relationships. This is far more than the usual humaneness of liberal arts education. If the values of the community are no more than the values of humanism, it is impossible to create the type of viable institution which is envisioned in this model.

From these basic statements, the institution can carefully articulate a statement of goals growing out of this philosophy. Some of these goals might include such statements as: It is the purpose of the institution to provide an atmosphere that is conducive to the Christian faith. It is equally the purpose of the institution to deal with the problems of the intellectual world which are raised by faith. One of the goals might be: It is the purpose of the institution to assist the student in the problems of maturation by use of the academic experience, by personal counseling, and by the atmosphere of Christian caring.

Christian Community

Crucial to the welfare of an institution such as is envisioned here, is the constant attempt to create and maintain a Christian community. The institution must seek to base the community on wisdom as well as freedom. There must be a deliberate choice by the community on self-limitations. It is certainly true that individual rights and institutional rights are important, and they must exist. But the community will consciously choose to limit the pursuits of rights in a legal sense in the favor of a free choice of a limited environment. Human rights pressed to a logical conclusion with each person exercising the limits of his constitutional powers will soon destroy a Christian community. It is internally disruptive, it is externally deadly. The community should choose certain limitations in order to exist and pursue superior goals and values.

The chief characteristics of the Christian community will have at least the following: There will be the caring for the concerns and needs of each member of the community by the other members of the community. If this spirit of caring is not readily forthcoming for the members of the community because of the nature of their own personal Christian commitment, it will nevertheless be exercised as one of the academic and spiritual requirements of being a member of the community. This caring will involve counseling in personal problems provided by both interested individuals and professionally trained people. The community will need to make available to needy students tutoring to help them in their academic deficiencies. Scholarship help must be available as it usually is, to help students who have financial need. Probably the prime characteristic in this community is an understanding that it is the responsibility as well as the privilege of each member of the community to be mutually helpful.

The involvements of this community mean that there must be

a commitment to a level of personal conduct that is not incompatible with the Christian community. Licentiousness, for example, has no place in such community, and would be destructive to the creation and maintenance of such community in an academic setting.

Let it be said that this is not to be construed as fuzzy sentimentalism. The Christian community involves the intelligent analysis of the situation, and the Christian decisions related to the various problems in the internal community will often involve steel in a velvet glove. The Christian community will inevitably involve some dismissals in order to maintain the integrity of the body. Christian requirements will certainly demand that academic work will have to be passed. There will be no gifts. The academic requirements should be designed to provide the best possible education to every student member of the community.

Administrative Officers

The administrative officers of such an institution will of necessity be committed Christians. They must be committed to the community, and to its ideals.

The president will need a profound understanding of the philosophy and goals of the college. There must be on his part an absolute commitment to them. This means, of course, he must be a deeply committed Christian, and he must be able to translate his Christian commitment into human relationships. The greatest need in daily administration by the president will be the factor of judgement. He will be endlessly involved with such questions as: What does a Christian act like under pressure? It will be necessary for him to demonstrate Christian conduct when the tensions are great, when there is external interference, when things do not go right in the community. He will be faced with the question: What is the Christian course in problems related to misconduct, the breakdown of the spirit of Christian community, and the normal tensions and disciplinary cases which an educational institution involves?

The academic dean in such an institution will be a most important post. This officer is crucial to the implementation of such plan. It is axiomatic that he must have a deep sense of personal

Christian commitment to the ideals and goals of the institution. He must have a desire to implement them in the academic life of the college, and be endlessly involved in attempting to determine what are the intellectual implications of these ideals and how do they speak to the community of scholars. In turn, how does the intellectual community affect the ideals of the institution. Complete intellectual honesty is one of the prime needs of this post. Without such an individual in the post of dean, it will be difficult if not impossible to implement such a program as this in the classroom.

Student personnel officers will be as crucial to this institution as to any other kind. Essentially they must be committed to Christian community. Their questions will involve such problems as: What is a Christian attitude toward youthful indiscretions? What kind of responsibility do we have to people with academic problems? What is the individual's attitude toward being the authority figure, and what are the problems in bearing the unchristian attitudes of students? These officers will need an ability to care about the total welfare of the individual. It is at the point of the student personnel officers where students will most often see manifest the nature of Christian community in the strictures that are necessary for the maintenance of this fellowship.

The key people in any educational institution, and no less in this idealized one, are faculty members. These members will have to be chosen with the nature of the institution in mind. Of course, there can be no coercion in matters of personal faith. These people will be selected because they are committed Christians, because they are interested in the presuppositions and in the theological bases of this community. Their personal limitations will be voluntarily accepted in the interest of creating and maintaining a Christian community.

These personal limitations, freely accepted, in no sense should prevent their exercise of their academic responsibilities. They will have complete freedom to explore, to inquire, to question, to discuss and to pursue knowledge wherever it may lead. There must be an openness and freedom in academic pursuits, including the necessity and the opportunity to criticize the community and its leaders. Constructive criticism should not be construed as being unchristian but rather a requirement for responsible participation in the community.

These people must be competent professionals. This requirement has serious implications for the Christian college. There is no substitute for competent professionals in the classroom. A Christian college can thrive with limited physical facilities. It must not present an inadequate educational experience to unsuspecting students paying high tuition and call it Christian. These are people who will have to face the intellectual problems of their discipline as these relate to Christian faith and the presuppositions upon which the institution is founded. Having honestly faced these intellectual problems, they must remain convinced of the viability of their Christian commitment. Thus they will be able to entertain questions and questioning. They will be able to accept the constant challenge of new knowledge, fads, and speculations, which are endlessly presented to the intellectual. It, of necessity, follows that they must be willing to bear the brunt of being professionally different and operating within a set of circumstances that will not coincide precisely with the other institutions with whom they have relationship.

The experienced educator will be concerned about the student role in such as idealized community as this.

The institution must be careful to set forth the nature of the uniqueness of the institution. Students who come are those who will be familiar with the motive of the institution and accept limitations necessary to protect it. Students will be acceptable if they accept the concept. There must be no coercion in matters of faith. According to our polity stipulated at the beginning of the model, these are people who are presumed to be competent in matters of faith. They have the right of direct access to God for themselves. They have the responsibility of formulating and stating their own understanding of the Christian faith, or their rejection of it if they so desire.

These will be students who will be interested in pursuing this orientation to life. It will be a matter of sharing faith and questions. Each will be left to accept or reject the interpretations of the institution as he chooses. There will be no rejection of students who do not accept this theology and philosophy, provided they are willing to live together in peace within the community. This will thus be a frankly ministering missionary community, not with the interest of proselyting students but with the interest of sharing with them the understanding of the Christian faith for which the institution itself stands.

This kind of institution and community will require the counseling of prospective students. Careful recruiting of individuals who are willing to live together in such mutual commitment will be necessary. Student controls will be oriented not toward monastic separation from society but in the maintenance of the nature of the institution. There will be no religious coercion, and there will be complete openness in the discussion of the problems which the community inevitably will create. Student control will be oriented toward the reasonable standard of personal conduct in order to protect the nature of the community and its constituency relationship. Thus membership in the community will not require belief but living together in a community that understands the nature of its commitment.

The nature of this institution must be so clearly set forth that the faculty and students entering it will know its nature. They will understand something of its commitment to its members and to its constituency. The institution is then obligated to protect and foster the uniqueness of the community, but there will be no requirement related to student acceptance of the theological bases of the community.

Denominational Relationships

There will need to be an understanding by all members of the community that a denomination has a right to create and to maintain an educational institution. This understanding will settle many of the problems from the outset related to constituency response to the difficulties of the institution. There are those in the educational community today who profess to believe that the sponsoring and/or creating body has no right to an interest in the affairs of the institution. The college of necessity must understand the nature of this relationship and be willing to live together in harmony with those who sponsor it. *The denomination has an obligation to support the institution if it exercises the right of control of the institution.*

In denominational relationships *the institution has the responsibility for communicating the true nature of the college.* It must make certain that the constituency understands its philosophy and goals. One of the problems concerning relationships with controlling constituency is that the institution has not made clear the nature of its problems. Complete openness with the denomination is essential. There must be a carefully articulated effort on the part of the institution to continue communications with the sponsoring body.

One college at the point of major problems internally or externally issued a pastor's newsletter sent to all the pastors of the state convention. These newsletters clearly set forth the nature of the problem, what was done about it, what could be expected from the difficulty in the future. It was of immeasurable value in stopping the endless rumors which arose related to a given problem.

It shall be the responsibility of the institution to cultivate the denomination. Criticisms from the denomination that are valid should be taken into consideration by the institution. Those that are invalid should be carefully explained in so far as this is possible, not only to denominational leadership but also to the rank and file of the denomination if means are available. If they are not available, means must be created if the institution is to enjoy the kind of relationship with the sponsoring denomination that is essential to achieve adequate support in these times.

The Christian community must be at pains to try to create the same sort of Christian attitudes towards the denomination that it tries to create internally. Criticisms of the denomination should be constructive in nature and Christian in tone.

Development Program

A strong development program—including a program of denominational relations, public relations to the many publics of the institution, the recruiting of students, cultivation of alumni, and financial involvement—is essential. The chief asset in the formulation of such a program is an atmosphere of confidence created by many of the factors already delineated in this paper. The atmosphere of confidence will depend on denominational relations, upon conditions within the school, upon attempts at Christian community. It will involve a thorough knowledge on the part of all parties concerned, particularly the director of development, of the goals of the institution and of the honest facing of the problems with which it is confronted.

The pressure of financial problems will undoubtedly grow. From outside sources many institutions presently match at least dollar-for-dollar funds received from fees and tuitions. Many go far beyond the one-for-one ratio. Denominational dollars are already inadequate to meet the needs of this kind of an institution, and present projections indicate that the share will diminish rather than increase.

It should be understood, however, that many people are interested in the kind of educational experience that is being here discussed. The development program of this institution will need to tell the story of the school. It will use all available means and methods. The story will need to be told personally to as many individuals as possible—by the president, the development director, and other members of the community.

OBU used a fund campaign approach to selling Christian higher education. Small financial campaigns for capital needs were organized at many carefully selected places in the state. Individuals were invited not to financial solicitation but to hear the story of the institution. Remarkable results were obtained as these people heard what the institution was attempting to accomplish. Considerable money was raised, but perhaps the most significant accomplishment was the ability to share the story of the institution with a growing number of those who would normally be interested in it and its future. This has obvious long-range benefits for the institution. As more and more people became knowledgeable about OBU's program, cooperative program gifts grew from $453,000 to one million, and ever-increasing sums have been raised for capital purposes. I am happy to give you this report entitled "Since I Left."

The educational program described in this paper is a saleable product in this kind of world. Christian people will support the kind of effort that is being described. This kind of institution is needed. Christian people are interested in it. They will accept its shortcomings and its failures if they understand the attempt that is being made. Students who understand it will want to attend this kind of an institution.

In this kind of world, build a better college and beat a path to the door of Christian constituents, and it can be sold.

Curriculum

The curriculum of this institution must be designed according to the purpose of the institution. It seems obvious that the principle thrust will be a liberal arts thrust. This fits with the nature of the institution, it fits with the historic position of this kind of school, and it meets the needs of the kinds of leaders that it will be the purpose of the school to produce.

"There must be relevancy to the modern world in order to equip young people to live in the world. There must be an open willingness to discuss the issues; educational, moral, ethical and spiritual which confront the student in his everyday life, and which confront the institution. This will require a high degree of intellectual honesty, and it will require a considerable amount of understanding on the part of the constituency. Many Baptist people still believe that their young people ought to be protected from alien ideas and from the confrontation with the world in which they must live. The curriculum of a Christian institution must meet the needs of young, growing, expanding minds as they are about to go into a world that is hostile basically to the faith which they hold. While it attempts this relevancy, it must also hold on to Christian values and the demands of Christian ethics and morality."

The recommendation of McKenzie and Patillo seems especially valuable related to the formulation of a world view. A world-view seminar may be required of all graduating seniors in such an institution as this in which an attempt is made at synthesis of knowledge. A world-view study should furnish the framework for the organization of knowledge. It should furnish the requirement of thinking about synthesis of knowledge. It would attempt to put together formally the requirements of science, social sciences, philosophy, religion, etc., in a comprehensive hold that would furnish the integration of knowledge not usually achieved accidentally or fortuitously. Such an effort should be very helpful in helping the student organize his college experience as it relates to his faith, as it relates to the physical world in which he lives and as it relates to himself and his human relationships.

Summary

More than ever before Christian colleges must decide what they are. They must face their theology and its implications in their philosophy. They must decide whom they wish to educate. They must state quite carefully what they are, and then see to it that the concept is widely publicized, particularly to those to whom they appeal for support. The Christian college must spend every effort to be what it claims to be. Its curricular offerings must furnish some assistance in helping the student understand what the institution says it is, and understand himself and his relationship to the world.

The Christian college must recognize its limitations. If it does not recognize its limitations as far as curricular offerings are concerned, it will be in an impossible situation financially. It cannot be all things to all people.

The Christian college should be on the leading edge of social, moral and ethical problems. Of necessity these efforts will be poorly understood. It will be difficult for the Christian college to articulate this effort and to sell it to its constitutents. Yet it is essential that the effort be made if it is going to accomplish the purposes for which it exists.

Inherent in the nature of this institution is the requirement that it attempt to teach people how to live together in peace while in open disagreement about ideas. What a contribution this would be to Baptist churches! This community must have the Christian requirement of openness and discussion and confrontation of ideas. This will prevent students from becoming "hot house plants." It can produce leaders who think, but leaders who feel as well. It should present to the churches of the denomination a constituency that will be competent to help in

the church and in the problems with which it is endlessly confronted. It should produce a lay leadership as well as professional leadership for the church communities that will have an
intellectual as well as a personal orientation to the problem filled
society in which it lives.

I am sure you recognize that this is a dynamic concept. It is
impossible to write rules for every set of circumstances which will
inevitably confront such an effort as this. The institution must
operate on the concept that it is a dynamic entity. It must strive
for creative Christian solutions to problems. As circumstances
change, so will adaptation to those circumstances. This will be a
problem-filled academic society. It will require endless discussion. Openness is basic. Christian commitment to caring will be a
central facet in it.

Some such formulation of the Christian academic ideals is
viewed by this author as being absolutely mandatory to the
maintenance of church-related higher education in such a society as we know. As I have tried to articulate an ideal for a
Christian college, I have honestly felt that I would like my
children to find such a school. I could in conscience support
such a venture. It would bring to its students the best of
academic and spiritual worlds. It would put Baptist polity to
work in the academic setting. This school would bring to the
faltering world a new vision of personal and academic excellence. This school would furnish a great place to spend a life.
Many of you labor in institutions that have some of these characteristics. God lets the lines of your lives fall in pleasant places. We
are at one of the most crucial points in the history of the
republic—you are at one of the most important opportunities
God has given to man. This is your grandest hour—God help
you to take advantage of it.